The Ocean City NJ Boardwalk

2½ Miles of Summer

2nd Edition

Dean Davis

Schiffer Publishing Ltd

4880 Lower Valley Road • Atglen, PA 19310

This book is dedicated to the three people who mean the most to me in the world: Sue, Jonathan, and Andrew. Without their love, support, and patience, this project never could have been possible.

Published by Schiffer Publishing Ltd.
4880 Lower Valley Road
Atglen, PA 19310
Phone: (610) 593-1777; Fax: (610) 593-2002
E-mail: Info@schifferbooks.com
www.schifferbooks.com

For our complete selection of fine books on this and related subjects, please visit our website at www.schifferbooks.com. You may also write for a free catalog.

Schiffer Publishing's titles are available at special discounts for bulk purchases for sales promotions or premiums. Special editions, including personalized covers, corporate imprints, and excerpts can be created in large quantities. For more information, contact the publisher.

We are always looking for people to write books on new and related subjects. If you have an idea for a book, please contact us at proposals@schifferbooks.com.

Contents

Acknowledgments

There are so many wonderful people to thank for their help with this project: my editors, Melissa and Tina, as well as the entire staff of Schiffer Publishing; my family, who has been carrying on the tradition of vacationing in Ocean City for many years; and the business owners, locals, and tourists of Ocean City.

Many people recognized my commitment to creating this book and gladly offered a helping hand. I'd like to thank them personally: Jim Laymon with his wonderful postcard collection and an unending knowledge about the boardwalk theaters; Hank Glaser of Shriver's who allowed me in his production room while he kept my children's pockets full of salt water taffy; Lori and George Steel of Steel's Fudge; Robin Habacht and Judi Vihonski from the Flanders Hotel; Larry and the awesome staff of the Ocean City Music Pier; Scott Simpson (a true wealth of information) and the crew at Playland's Castaway Cove; John W. Stauffer of Johnson's Popcorn; Janet Galante of Galante's Bikes and Surreys; Chuck Bangle and the staff of Manco and Manco Pizza; and Lisa Whitley of Fralinger's Original Salt Water Taffy.

A very special thank you goes to John Kavchok from Gillian's Wonderland Pier and Sean Zwiebel of Gillian's Island Water Park and Adventure Golf. These two gentlemen, as well as the entire Gillian's staff, went above and beyond my requests. Thank you so much, guys. I truly appreciate it.

I also want to acknowledge and thank Rich Updike, Terri Davis, Sean Davis, and Matt Webb for bringing their photographic skills to this book. Terri, who helped with the Flanders and Shriver's shoots, thank you very much for your assistance. Rich, I wish you could be here, my friend, to share in the joy of the finished product. Thanks also go to Helen Updike and her son, Christopher, for giving me permission to use Rich's

Rich Updike
Photo courtesy of Helen Updike

photos. And lastly, my thanks go to Sue Davis and Mary Jane Arden, who had to sit through my many sessions of photo selection and manuscript reading.

This book is a result of my love for the boardwalk and all the wonderful memories it holds for me. Riding a surrey in the early morning hours, dropping some quarters in the arcade, walking the boards, watching my twins laugh on the rides, lounging on the beach, watching the yo-yo champs on Family Nights, and considering a bucket of Jilly's fries as a meal are all things I consider part of my summer ritual. Each family has their own favorite restaurant, hotel or motel, amusement spots and activities, but most can agree that there's no other place like the Ocean City Boardwalk.

Rich Updike had a photographer's eye. Something would catch his attention and he would snap a picture at just the right second. In other instances, he would patiently wait out a shot on the freezing beach to capture just the right feel or event. No matter what the circumstance, Rich would come away with a beautiful photo.

I first met Rich when my wife, Sue, and I stayed at the Flanders just prior to New Year's Eve 2004. We arrived late in the evening and were greeted by a kind, white-haired gentleman at the front desk. He said, "My name is Rich and anything you need help with, just give me a call." I didn't realize then how prophetic his words would be.

Schiffer Publishing had just contracted me to do this title. We took this trip so I could make contact with some of the businesses and get a few pictures. After checking in, my wife stayed in the room and I went back down to the lobby. My intent was to get a name or two regarding the Flanders' history and permission for a photo shoot. Rich jotted down the info and then we started to talk about the book.

"I took that picture," he said as he pointed to a brochure on the counter, "and I took those too."

Our conversation quickly moved to photography and Rich's work. He explained that he rarely took pictures with people in them. He preferred the beauty of nature and landscapes. He also liked taking pictures of birds. By living in the Ocean City area Rich and his camera gave us a perspective that many don't get to see, the boardwalk and beach in the dead of winter. I invited Rich to be a part of the book, but first I had to work out some legalities and logistics.

Sue and I returned to the Flanders during Valentine's Day weekend. Rich was excited about being part of the book and told me he would send a sample disc of images. His work was incredible. He truly captured the beauty of Ocean City and its beaches.

In talking with Rich I learned that he had a lifelong goal to visit every state in the Union. At this point in his life, he had already visited forty-eight of them and had two to go. He was finalizing his travel plans to Alaska; Hawaii would be after that. I wished him well and told him I would be contacting him in regards to the book in the coming months.

When photography was scheduled to begin in the late spring I phoned Rich. It was then that I heard the news. Rich passed away April 2, 2005. He did visit Alaska, but he never made it to Hawaii. His widow, Helen, was extremely cooperative and with the help of their son, Christopher, she sent me Rich's portfolio. I'm truly grateful for that gesture and I'm happy to give Rich's work the exposure it deserves.

Photos courtesy of Rich Updike

A Quick History

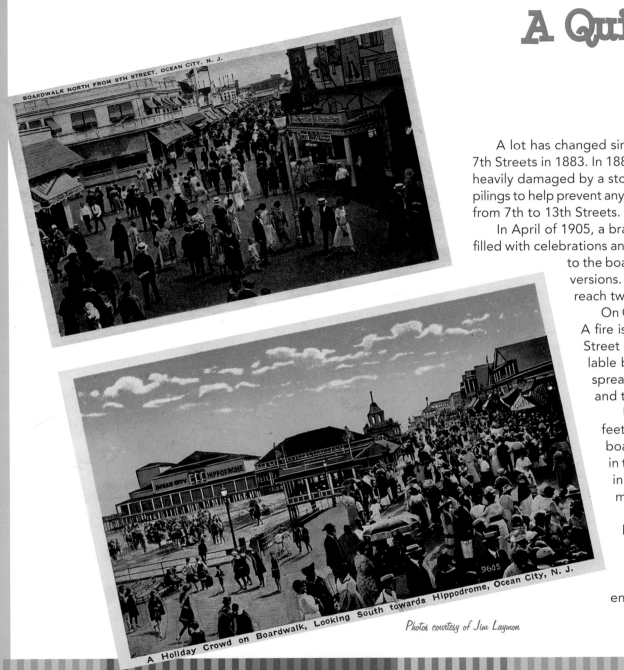

BOARDWALK NORTH FROM 9TH STREET, OCEAN CITY, N. J.

A Holiday Crowd on Boardwalk, Looking South towards Hippodrome, Ocean City, N. J.

Photos courtesy of Jim Laymon

A lot has changed since the boardwalk was first constructed between 4th and 7th Streets in 1883. In 1887, the boardwalk was expanded to 11th Street, but it was heavily damaged by a storm the following year. In 1889, it was rebuilt with cement pilings to help prevent any further storm damage. At this time the boardwalk stretched from 7th to 13th Streets.

In April of 1905, a brand new two-mile boardwalk was dedicated. The day was filled with celebrations and festivities. This boardwalk was raised off the sand similar to the boardwalk we know today. It was also wider than the previous versions. Further expansion took place over the years that would reach two and a half miles upon completion.

On October 11, 1927, the boardwalk faced its biggest disaster. A fire is believed to have started in a pile of trash under the 9th Street part of the boardwalk and quickly grew into an uncontrollable blaze. Strong winds from the southeast caused the fire to spread quickly. Larger buildings were consumed by the flames and the boardwalk was destroyed for blocks.

Upon reconstruction, the boardwalk was moved about 300 feet closer to the ocean. Its design incorporated the latest boardwalk engineering technologies, which made it the finest in the country at that time. Two other storms of note occurred in 1944 and 1962, requiring that the boardwalk undergo major reconstruction.

For generations, families have enjoyed "walking the boards" on cool summer nights. Parents cherish the memories of watching their children enjoy the amusement piers. Eventually these same children are given a curfew when they are old enough to hang out with their friends and enjoy the boardwalk from a whole new angle.

The boardwalk in the early 1900s had a few distinct turns in it, unlike the mainly straight run that exists today.

Finding a spot on the beach was never really a problem in the fledgling days of the boardwalk. *Photo courtesy of Jim Laymon*

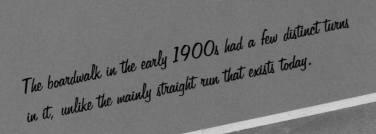

BIRDSEYE VIEW OF STEEPLE CHASE PIER & BOARDWALK, OCEAN CITY, N. J.

The Boardwalk in 1941. At the right is the entrance to the terminus for the train line to Atlantic City. *Photo courtesy of Jim Laymon*

TERMINUS AT BOARDWALK AND EIGHTH ST.
OCEAN CITY

Scene along lines of Atlantic City & Shore Railroad, between Atlantic City and Ocean City

This shows how close we are to the boardwalk

The Atlantic City and Shore Railroad ran between Atlantic City and Ocean City. The end of the line would bring you right up to the steps of the boardwalk on 8th Street. In 1948, the rail service was discontinued. *Photo courtesy of Jim Laymon*

The Golden Galleon building as it appeared in the 1970s. Gino's was a burger chain started by members of the Baltimore Colts in 1957. The space occupied by the Copper Kettle eventually became Fralinger's Original Salt Water Taffy. The area under the sign was reconstructed into a doorway for Fralinger's. *Photo courtesy of Jim Laymon*

Boardwalk above 8th Street, Ocean City, N. J.

Photos courtesy of Jim Laymon

You can see how fashions on the boardwalk have changed over the decades. The above postcard is from sometime before the 1927 fire; the other is from 1964. There were various laws during the early part of the 20th century dictating what was deemed appropriate as beach and boardwalk attire. One of the odder laws that lasted until the late 1940s stated that all males had to wear shirts while on the beach.

On the Boards

The "official" start of the Ocean City Boardwalk.

At every quarter mile on the boardwalk there is a marker.

This incredible view allows you to see from the Wonderland Pier all the way down to the Port-O-Call Hotel.
Photo by Rich Updike

Looking down towards 1st Street near the Ocean City Beach Patrol Station.

12

The Ocean City Music Pier is the largest structure on the beach side of the boardwalk. Located at Moorlyn Terrace, it was built after the 1927 fire and has been in the same spot for more than seventy-five years. Despite some storm damage and technological upgrades over the years, little has changed within the Music Pier.

City Pier - Ocean City, N. J.

Photo courtesy of Jim Laymon

The original Municipal Music Pavilion, also known as the City Pier, was built in 1905 to house free concerts and entertainment. Standing where the current Music Pier is, this building survived the 1927 fire and was moved to Sixth Street. It was also renamed Convention Hall and hosted many varied types of events until fire claimed it in 1965.

Work on the Music Pier began in 1928, and was dedicated on July 4th of 1929. A large parade and fireworks were a part of the celebration. Standing on more than one hundred concrete pilings, it rises twenty feet above the sand. The large dance floor measured 60 x 85 feet.

Soon after the Japanese attack on Pearl Harbor, a temporary observation tower was built on the roof of the Music Pier. It was the first structure in the United States constructed exclusively for the observation and spotting of possible enemy planes flying along the coast. Volunteers of all ages and genders manned the tower during the war years.

Many events are held inside the great hall, which can seat 1,100 concert-goers. The Ocean City Pops call the Music Pier home as they continue to bring cultured music to the sandy shores. World-renowned performers such as Shirley Jones and Joel Grey occasionally grace the Music Pier's stage. Each season many venture to the Music Pier to enjoy an evening of relaxing entertainment.

Consider the boardwalk a two-and-a-half-mile outdoor mall. There are plenty of retail offerings. You can purchase the latest beach fashions, jewelry, antiques, and even kites. If you want something to eat, there is no shortage of choices.

I see a pleasant vacation in your near future, but only if you use SPF 30 sunscreen.

There is a legend of a beach chair that was chained to a railing on the boardwalk. It seems the owner of the chair would leave it there all beach season and use it as needed. Instead of carrying it home, he or she would lock it up. No one ever stole it, and during the off-season the chair would be gone. The location varied between the ramps on 8th and 9th streets but the basis of the story was always the same. While photographing this book, the mysterious chair was never seen, but there were plenty of other things padlocked to the railings of the boardwalk.

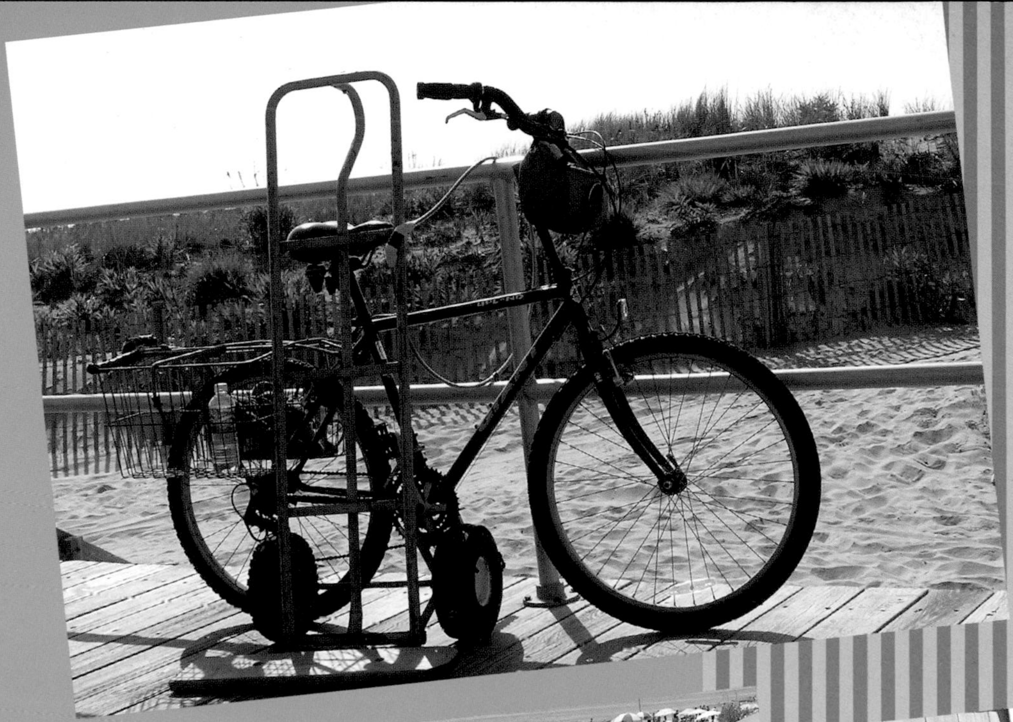

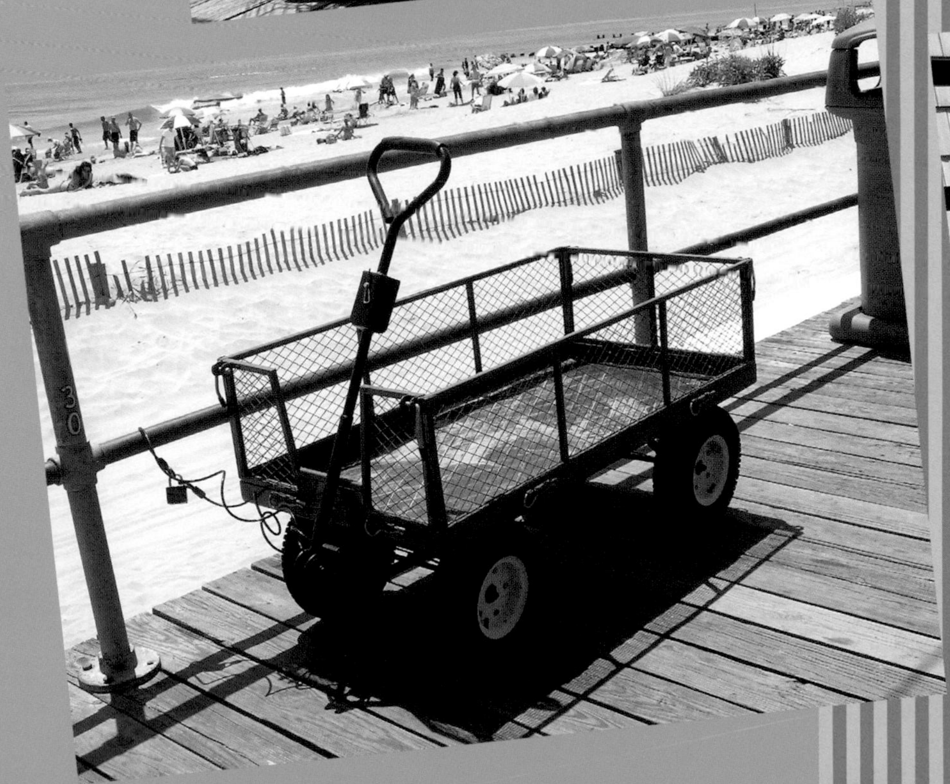
30

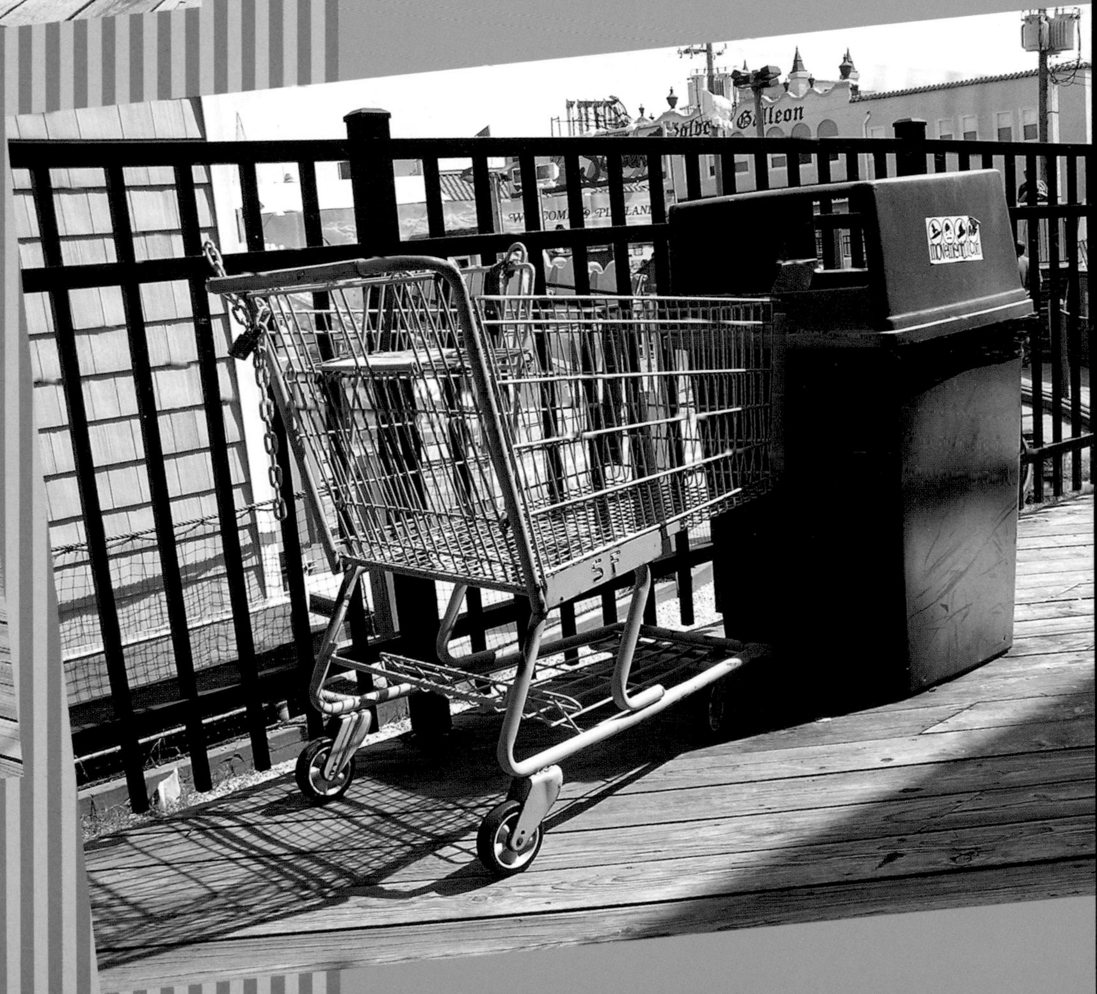
Galleon
SF

The Flanders is the grand old hotel of Ocean City which opened her doors on July 28th, 1923. It was named after Flanders Field in Belgium, a World War I cemetery for many American soldiers. The intent of the Ocean Front Hotel Corporation was to create a seaside resort that would rival some of the finest hotels in the major cities. The builders offered $100-a-point stock investment to members of the community as a means to help support the venture.

The architect was Ocean City native Vivian Smith who was well known for his Atlantic City and Philadelphia buildings. He also designed Ocean City Hall and Ocean City High School. At the time, the Flanders was the biggest construction project ever undertaken inside the borders of the small resort town. The end result was everything the investors envisioned.

Built in the Spanish Mission Revival Style, it was originally right up against the boardwalk. After the 1927 fire the boardwalk moved forward, but the Flanders stayed put. The hotel is well known for its elegant weddings and receptions held in the grand and spacious rooms. Jimmy Stewart, Grace Kelly, and cartoonist Al Capp are some of the celebrities who have visited the Flanders.

J. Howard Slocum was the original manager of the Flanders. His previous experience was with the Waldorf Astoria and other noted hotels. Slocum held a national marbles tournament at the Flanders to publicize its opening. The exposure in many newspapers was great publicity for the hotel.

The stock market crash of 1929 took a huge toll on the Flanders. By 1932, it was sold to Elwood F. Kirkman. Even though times were hard, Kirkman maintained the first-class accommodations. He lived at the Flanders to constantly keep an eye on the business. Kirkman remained the owner for more than forty years until his death.

Along with the indoor luxuries, the outdoor attractions were just as glamorous in the hotel's heyday. The Flanders boasted four spectacular swimming pools as well as tennis courts and other recreational amenities for its patrons. One of the pools took up most of the space where Castaway Cove's outdoor amusement area operates today.

Swimming meets, water polo matches, and diving shows were held in those pools. The Ocean City Beach Patrol held water saving demonstrations and similar events for more than fifty years at the Flanders. The tennis courts were in the spot where the log flume in Castaway Cove is currently located.

Debts and hard times plagued the Flanders during the late 1980s and early '90s. James M. Dwyer purchased the landmark hotel in 1996. The rooms were remodeled and some were transformed into condominiums. Grand weddings, events, and vacationers fill the Flanders during most of the year as the hotel has proudly returned to much of its original grandeur.

Photo by Terri Davis

The grand hallway on the Flanders' second floor.
Photo by Terri Davis

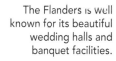

The Flanders is well known for its beautiful wedding halls and banquet facilities.

The Flanders had a large salt water pool. It was located on what is now the south side of Castaway Cove.

The Flanders is built in the Spanish Mission Revival Style. In searching all around the building you can find various architectural accents that give the Flanders its unique charm.

24

IS THE FLANDERS HAUNTED?

Some believe a ghost walks among the halls of the Flanders Hotel. A pleasant spirit given the name Emily has been spotted in the hotel over the years. Nothing is known of her past, but witnesses describe her as a girl in her early twenties with long brown hair. She wears a flowing white dress and is barefoot as she strolls through the walls. Her gentle singing and laughter has awoken more than a few guests. Locks have been played with and light bulbs have become mysteriously unscrewed in their fixtures. Her main "haunts" appear to be the grand banquet rooms and the hall of mirrors. Another favorite place for sightings is near the grand piano on the second floor. A large painting of Emily is displayed in that area, with her features based on descriptions given by those who have seen her. If you ever stay at the Flanders make sure you look for the young lady in the white dress singing songs from another place and time.

Some days it's just best to sit on a bench and
do some people watching.

Lanes are marked for the morning activities along the Boardwalk. Pedestrians use the outer lanes.

The Ocean City Beach Patrol Station located at 12th and Boardwalk.

Nothing beats an evening of walking on the boardwalk.

Photo by Sean Davis

Litterer's has been on the boardwalk for decades. They were always famous for their orange juice. On August 10, 2002, a fire nearly wiped out this boardwalk landmark. Stewart's Root Beer and several other businesses also sustained heavy damage.

The origin of the fire appeared to be a cigarette that was discarded under the boardwalk and ignited some trash. In December of 2002, Ocean City council members voted to designate smoking areas along the boardwalk in an effort to prevent future fires. The businesses affected by the fire are back on the boards and proudly serving customers.

O – Manco & Manco, C – Antique Cars (Castaway Cove), E – Congo Falls Water Ice, A – The Islander, N – Wonderland, C – Castaway Cove, I – The Riptide (Castaway Cove), T – The Strand, Y – Goofy Golf

Movie theaters have been present on the boardwalk since the silver screen captured the country's imagination back in the early 20th century. Some were originally built to house all forms of entertainment, including vaudeville, but eventually they showed movies full-time. The Moorlyn and the Strand Theaters in Ocean City were owned by members of the Shriver family, of Shriver's Salt Water Taffy fame, for many years.

The Moorlyn Theater opened as a bowling alley on the boardwalk between 8th and 9th Streets in the early 1900s. A huge dance hall occupied the second floor and had a stage for the band. Large windows would allow a gentle ocean breeze to cool off the dancers.

Sometime around the early 1920s, the floor was angled, a stage was added on the first floor, and the bowling alleys were disassembled. During this period the name of the establishment ceased to be Moore's Bowling Casino and became the Moorlyn Theater. The Moorlyn miraculously escaped damage from the 1927 fire. After the new boardwalk was built closer to the beach, the Moorlyn stayed back one block for a year before it was brought up to the boardwalk.

During the mid-century, the exterior was changed as the upstairs ballroom windows were covered, and a neon marquee was added. During the 1970s the 2,000-seat theater was divided into a twin theater, the first on the boardwalk.

The Moorlyn Theater in the summer of 1962. *Photo courtesy of Jim Laymon*

The original Strand Theater was located between Moorlyn Terrace and 9th Street on the boardwalk. The lobby was known to be very upscale and even included fresh-cut flowers. It survived the 1927 fire, but then burned down in the fall of 1937.

The Shriver family decided to rebuild the Strand at the corner of 9th and Boardwalk. It was to be the finest boardwalk theater in the county. Their goals and dreams were fulfilled with the opening on August 11th, 1938, of a new and elegant 1,450-seat Strand Theater. Luxuries included twin balconies, blue glass block in the lobby that was imported from Belgium, and air-conditioning.

The debut movie was *Give Me a Sailor* starring Bob Hope and Martha Raye. Adult matinee tickets cost forty-five cents with the evening show charging a fifty-five cent admission. Total attendance that first day was 1,539.

Except for the addition of a candy stand, the building remained unchanged for fifty years. The theater kept its Art Deco look until 1989, when the theater was sold. It was chopped up into five small theaters and none of the classic interior was retained.

The old theater is now the Surf Mall.

The Showboat eventually became the Surf.

The Showboat Theater as it was in 1929.
Photo courtesy of Jim Laymon

The Showboat Theater was built on 12th and Boardwalk soon after the 1927 fire. It was advertised as Ocean City's only fireproof theater. Back then, "fireproof" was a big selling point for new structures. The Flanders Hotel was advertised as a fireproof hotel even before the devastating fire of 1927.

Sometime during its life the theater's name was changed to the Surf after the Showboat sign blew down in a storm. Legend (or rumor) has it that it was cheaper to spell Surf as opposed to Showboat. During the late 1970s, the building was in bad shape. The first few rows were permanently roped off because of standing water resulting from damage to the roof. Around 1979, the theater stopped showing movies and fell victim to neglect. Today the theater has been revived into a shopping marketplace.

Each year thousands of people enjoy the Ocean City beaches.

There are plenty of adventurous activities in Ocean City. Parasailing is just one of them.

New surfers take lessons as more experienced ones enjoy the waves in the early morning sun. *Photo by Sean Davis.*

A new day dawns over the Music Pier. *Photo by Rich Updike*

Photo by Rich Updike

Many youngsters experience the beach for the first time in Ocean City.

For those who don't like to carry a lot to the beach, there are daily rental options.

Wooden sand fences help retain sand needed for a healthy sand dune ecosystem while planting vegetation reduces the impact of wind and water at high tide. *Photo by Sean Davis.*

You can find a large and varied bird population in Ocean City and the surrounding areas. Many different species inhabit the coastal region, and Southern New Jersey is a favorite spot for bird watchers. Getting involved in the hobby of bird watching is relatively easy. All you need is a good pair of binoculars, a bird identification guide, and the proper clothing if you decide to venture out into the wetlands and wooded areas.

Photos by Rich Updike

Photos by Rich Updike

46

This series of photos was taken from a second floor window in the Ocean City Music Pier. It was a combination of luck and being in the right place at the right time that allowed me to capture these shots.

48

This sandy masterpiece will be washed away sometime
during the night as the tide comes in.

Photo by Rich Updike

The Ocean City Beach Patrol has a long and illustrious reputation on the sandy shores of New Jersey. What started out in the late 1890s, as one man who took donations to patrol a small stretch of the beach, has expanded to a seasonal workforce numbering more than one hundred people. The OCBP has won numerous lifeguard competitions and races.

One of the prominent families associated with the OCBP is the Kelly family. John B. Kelly owned a vacation home on 26th Street where his family would spend their summers. Mr. Kelly was a world-class athlete and won several Olympic gold medals in the sport of sculling (rowing). He was a strong supporter and advocate for the OCBP. His son, Jack Jr., became an OCBP lifeguard in the 1940s, and won many competitions. The Kellys had a daughter named Grace who became a famous movie star and eventually a princess after she married Prince Rainier of Monaco.

The men and women of the OCBP have kept swimmers safe for more than one hundred years. In 2005, Ocean City was featured on ESPN as a national audience watched the OCBP win a major lifeguard competition.

The rules of the beach and boardwalk are clearly posted in Ocean City.

WELCOME TO OCEAN CITY

BEACH TAGS REQUIRED
9:30AM TO 5:30PM

PERSONS NOT PERMITTED ON BEACHES
10PM TO 6AM

NO BICYCLES ON BOARDWALK 12NOON TO 5AM

PROHIBITED ON BEACH OR BOARDWALK

DOGS | PICKNICKING ALCOHOLIC BEVERAGES | OPEN FIRES ORD. | LOUD MUSIC 87-17 | BALL OR FRISBEE THROWING | SKAT BOAR

DANGER

KEEP OFF JETTY

WARNING NO SWIMMING OR WADING

WITHOUT LIFEGUARD ON DUTY

ORD. 87-17

Set up some shade and enjoy a whole day at the beach.

Photos by Rich Updike

The Ocean City Fishing Club is located on a pier at 14th and Boardwalk. *Photo by Rich Updike*

Photo by Rich Updike

As the sun goes down and the beach crowd gets ready for dinner,
the extreme sportsmen emerge to take on the waves of Ocean City.

Photos by Rich Updike

Mr. David Gillian first arrived in Ocean City in 1914 as a musician in the various theaters and dance halls around town. The 1927 fire changed Mr. Gillian's career path when the theater where he was employed burned down. Noticing a lack of amusements on the rebuilt boardwalk, David Gillian opened up the Fun Deck at Plymouth Place and Boardwalk in 1930. Two of the main attractions were a Ferris Wheel and a Merry-Go-Round. Sixty years later in 1990, David Gillian celebrated his 100th birthday by donating a wooden horse from the original Merry-Go-Round to the Ocean City Historical Museum.

In 1957, David Gillian retired, and the business was handed over to his sons, Robert and Roy. In 1965 Roy left the family business and started the Wonderland Pier on the site of the old Stainton's Playland at 6th Street and Boardwalk. The new amusement area consisted of ten rides and a parking lot. It has grown quite a bit since then. The modern Ferris Wheel provides the best aerial view of the boardwalk and Ocean City.

Roy Gillian went into politics, and in 1985 was elected mayor of Ocean City. He has since left public office and is now an active member of the International Association of Amusements Parks and Attractions. A third generation of Gillian family members is now assisting in the operations of the various businesses.

Kids and adults alike enjoy the wholesome entertainment and large selection of rides and amusements Wonderland Pier has to offer. Group rates and birthday packages are available for the Wonderland Pier as well as a pre-season ticket sale in the spring.

Wonder Bear is the official mascot of Wonderland Pier. There is also a selection of Wonder Bear souvenirs.

The Twister will turn and spin
you in a thrill-filled ride.

The modern Fun Deck pays homage to David Gillian and his original amusement area at Plymouth Place and Boardwalk.

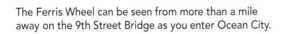

The Ferris Wheel can be seen from more than a mile away on the 9th Street Bridge as you enter Ocean City.

Photo by Rich Updike

Make sure you don't eat a lot before going on some of these rides.

During the morning hours, bikes and surreys are permitted on the boardwalk. Riders must pedal in their designated lanes. There are a few businesses within a block of the boardwalk where you can rent a variety of bikes and surreys.

Galante's Bikes and Surreys on 10th Street and Ocean Avenue is housed in the building that formerly served as a storage garage for the Flanders Hotel.

Gillian's Island Waterpark is a great place to splash and slide the day away. You can take a lazy, drifting ride while sitting on a tube, or you can propel your body down the twists and turns of their waterslides. Either choice is a refreshing way to cool off from the heat.

The lines may get long for some of the slides, but it is always worth the wait.

Li'l Buc's Bay is a place for the toddlers to have fun with water slides built to suit their size.

The Serpentine Slides are one of the waterpark's most popular attractions.

Feel the speed of the Shotgun Falls as you race down this slide.

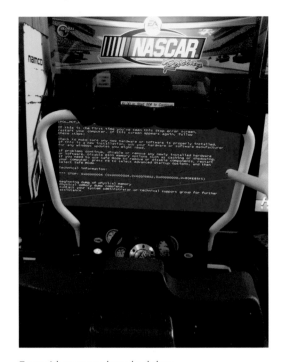

Even video games have bad days.

How FAST is YOUR FASTBALL

Go-Karting is always a favorite activity on the boardwalk.

Skeeball and the boardwalk were made for each other.

Dance Dance Revolution is one of those things that you can't miss on the boardwalk. Whether you're one of the dancers burning the calories and working up a sweat as you time your steps to the arrows on the screen, or an observer who enjoys watching the spectacle, this is truly a sight to see.

"DDR Freaks," as they are known, are stomping in arcades around the world as they try to master the routines and songs. The arcade phenomenon was first introduced in 1998 at the Tokyo Game Show in Japan. In Europe the game is known as Dancing Stage.

74

There are plenty of rides to choose from at Playland's Castaway Cove.

Playland's Castaway Cove is located on 10th Street and Boardwalk. With more than thirty rides to choose from, there is something for everyone's taste. Whether it's a roller coaster or a relaxing ride on a miniature train, every member of the family will have a good time.

Back in 1941, the amusement area opened under the name of Bingham's. The large arch building, which still stands today, was part of the 1939-40 World's Fair that was held in New York. After the fair was over, the building was dismantled and shipped to Ocean City where it was rebuilt and housed Bingham's.

In 1959, David Simpson and Fred Tarves purchased the business from the Bingham family and renamed the area Playland. There were eighteen rides within the building and on an outside deck. The amusements were mainly Allan Herschell brand kiddie rides, since Playland had to follow an odd law that stated no ride could be powered by a motor greater than one horsepower.

Mr. Tarves left Playland in 1972 to concentrate on his construction projects and Shoemaker Lumber, a lumberyard he owned in Ocean City. Playland was now a family-run business solely handled by the Simpsons. David Simpson's son, Scott, started working at Playland as a youth back in the late 1960s, and is currently handling the daily operations.

The biggest change to Playland came in 1996, when a huge expansion took place. Elwood F. Kirkman, the owner of the Flanders, passed away and the family sold much of the unused land in parcels. What was the large swimming area and tennis courts, abandoned years before, became the newly enlarged Playland's Castaway Cove.

Even though the rides and the layout have changed over the years, there is still a feeling of fun and family entertainment. They offer birthday party packages and their tickets never expire.

Bumper cars are always a popular choice with children of all ages.

A working miniature steam locomotive takes riders on a tour around the park.

The High Seas Log Flume provides a splashing good time...
when it is filled with water.

The brightly painted swings are truly a visual treat.
There are many artistic gems if you look close enough.

The Merry-Go-Round is a timeless classic.

The best roller coasters in Ocean City can be found at Playland's Castaway Cove.

Miniature golf is one of those things that almost everyone has participated in at least once while visiting Ocean City. The boardwalk abounds with courses to putt the time away. Some courses are easy and fun, while others add a true challenge to the game with their twisting and sometimes frustrating greens.

A chimp in a grass skirt and bikini top can fluster even the calmest golfer.

A general rule in miniature golf is the person closest to the hole after the first stroke goes first.

Daytime rates for a round of golf are cheaper at most places than evening hour rates.

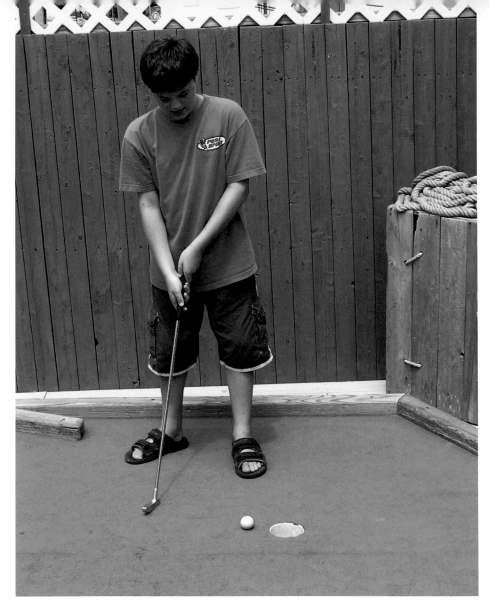

A good stance and a smooth swing will get you in the cup every time.

This old salt keeps an eye on the ocean from the roof of Playland's Seaport Village Golf.

Photo by Matt Webb

Some courses have ramps and obstacles, but a good golfer keeps his head in the game.

Fifty-four umbrellas keep the sun out of your eyes at the Area 51 Food Court.

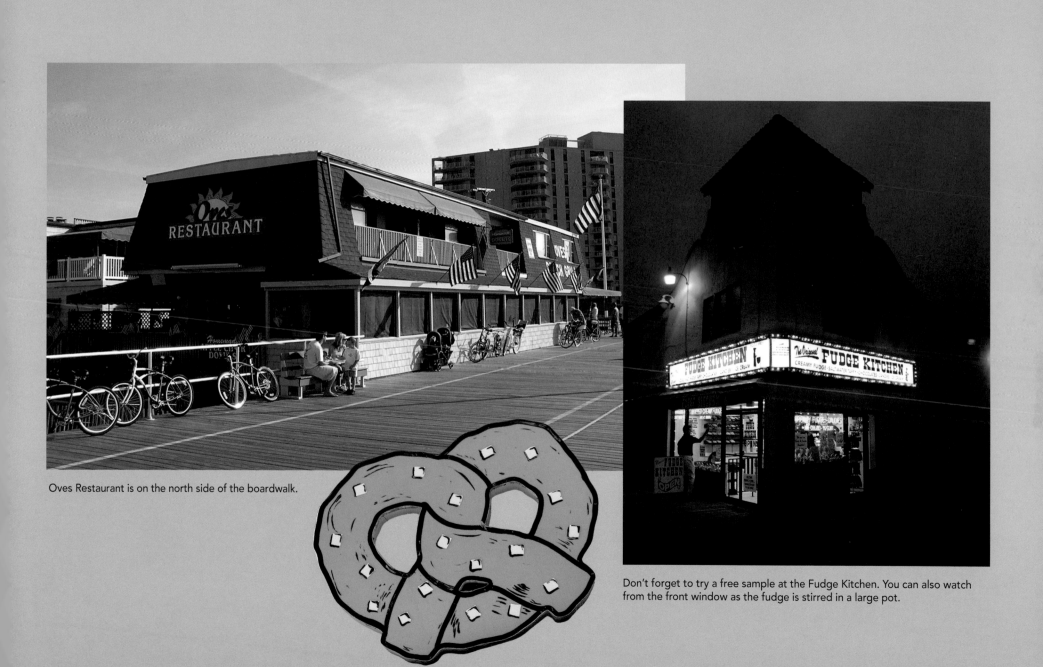

Oves Restaurant is on the north side of the boardwalk.

Don't forget to try a free sample at the Fudge Kitchen. You can also watch from the front window as the fudge is stirred in a large pot.

Photo by Sean Davis

Shriver's has been satisfying those with a sweet tooth for more than one hundred years. They're easily the oldest business on Ocean City's Boardwalk. William Shriver Sr. established the candy shop in 1898. The original building was destroyed in the 1927 fire and was rebuilt on the corner of 9th and Boardwalk.

The original Shriver's building before the 1927 fire. *Photo courtesy of Jim Laymon*

Shriver's makes all their fudge and salt water taffy right on the premises. One batch of fudge produces eighty pounds of creamy goodness. There are twenty-four salt water taffy flavors to choose from, while experimentation for new ones is an ongoing process.

As the taffy is being pulled, workers dust on starch so the taffy doesn't stick to the machines. The pulling of the taffy puts air into it and that's what makes the taffy chewy. Holes are occasionally poked in the taffy to release some of the trapped air. A batch is about fifty pounds. When the taffy is sliced, each batch yields about 2,000 pieces. Machines individually wrap each piece at a rate of about 450 pieces per minute. Some of the wrapped pieces are then packed in various sized boxes by hand. A one-pound box is comprised of forty-two to forty-four pieces. You can also mix and match your favorite flavors since Shriver's has bins of each flavor for custom choosing.

Huge windows are in the back of the store so you can watch the packaging process. The taffy machines are right up front beyond these windows, and fresh batches are made daily during the busy summer season. Shriver's offers many other tasty confections like macaroons and flavored mints.

Hank Glaser and his sister, Ginny Berwick, bought the business from their father in 1983, and have been running it ever since. The Glaser family has been associated with Shriver's since 1959.

Taffy being pulled at Shriver's. *Photo by Terri Davis*

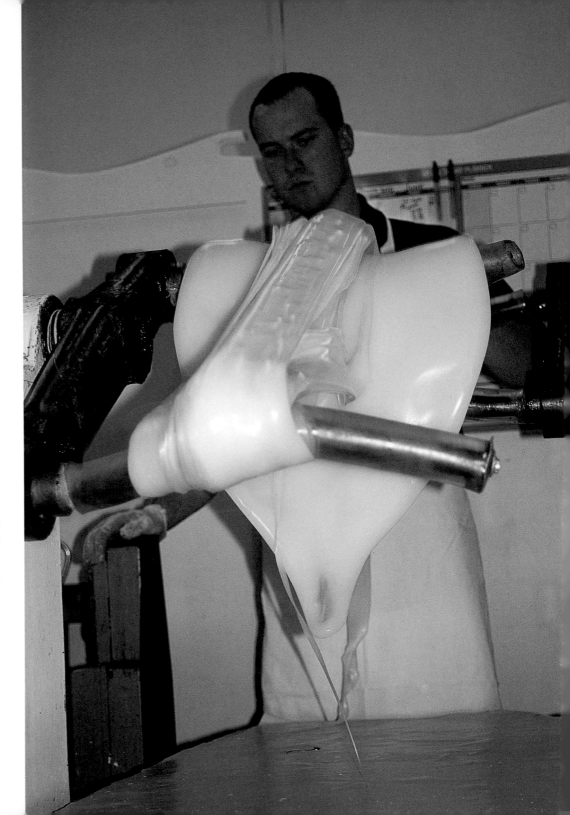

The taffy is machine wrapped.

Photo by Terri Davis

The fudge is made on the premises at Shriver's. *Photo by Terri Davis*

The fudge is poured into pans and left on shelves to harden. *Photo by Terri Davis*

The trays of fudge are then brought out front to the sales floor.

Shriver's offers many different kinds of sweet treats.

You never know what you'll find at Shriver's.

Don't forget to say hello to Mr. Taffy.

Pizza is a large part of the boardwalk's food pyramid. There are plenty of places to get a good slice along the boards. One of the favorite spots for vacationers is Manco & Manco (formerly Mack & Manco). They have been on the Ocean City boardwalk in some form or another since the summer of 1956. As with everything, change happens, but the great taste has remained. Years ago, Italian beachgoers called it tomato pie, but over the years the preferred name of "pizza" became the norm.

The pizza makers toss the dough right in front of the patrons.

Eventually, the children of Mack and Manco joined and expanded the business. They now have three locations in Ocean City. Families for generations have returned to watch the pizza makers throw the dough high. That's one tradition Manco & Manco has maintained over the years, making the pizzas fresh in front of the customers. Loyal patrons have consistently voted for Manco & Manco in many "Best of…" surveys. Some still call it "tomato pie," most call it pizza, but all call it delicious.

Steel's Fudge is the oldest family owned business on the Ocean City Board-walk. It was founded in 1919, when Elizabeth and Howard Steel opened up their shop in Atlantic City. The delicious fudge was a favorite with vacationers, and Steel's was one of the first businesses to feature fudge as its main attraction. For a boardwalk parade, Steel's made an incredibly large piece of fudge that had to be rolled on one of the wicker boardwalk push carts that can be found in Atlantic City.

The Ocean City location opened in 1949 at 736 Boardwalk. The business moved a few more times until 1972, when it came to its current location at 10th and Boardwalk. As a youngster, George Steel appeared as a contestant in the famed Ocean City Baby Parade. His float named him, "King of the Boardwalk," an event he's reminded of even to this day when he labors as a third-generation fudge maker.

The little ones love to pick from the many selections of candy while the older folks find it hard to choose which of the sixteen flavors fudge will make the trip home (if it lasts that long). Flavors change every now and then based on experimentation and public demand, but the rich goodness has remained constant. Steel's has also been featured on the Food Network, when the sweet treats were shown to a national audience.

The management and staff of Steel's welcome you to try any of their fabulous sixteen flavors of fudge.

Photo by Terri Davis

Johnson's Popcorn started in the 1920s in Philadelphia. They opened shops in Wildwood, and in 1940, opened up the Ocean City location. The crunchy treat was always a favorite with vacationers.

In 1974, John W. Stauffer and his wife, Rita, were both teaching abroad and were looking to come back to teach in New Jersey and get involved in a side business to occupy the summer months. They found an ad in the *Ocean City Sentinel-Ledger* pertaining to the sale of a boardwalk business. The ad in question was placed by Bill Keller, who was the owner of Johnson's Popcorn. He sold the Stauffers the business in August of 1974. It consisted of one popper and three pots to mix the caramel.

The first official season under the Stauffer's management started in the spring of 1975. In the mid-'80s, the Stauffers took on a partner, William M. Lombard, and opened up a second location. The third location opened in the mid-'90s. The recipe for Johnson's popcorn is so secretive that each employee must sign a contract never to reveal it upon hiring.

The process is very labor intensive and the work is all done by hand. Only large kernels are used in a sifting process that weeds out the smaller ones. The kernels are then air-popped. The caramel is stirred in the large copper kettles. It takes about eight minutes to make two and a half large tubs of popcorn. Back when he bought the business, the popcorn was only sold in bags, so John Stauffer came up with the Stay-Fresh Tub, which is still used today. Johnson's is open year-round at their 1360 Boardwalk location.

In 1917, the Kohr brothers wanted to expand their family dairy business, so they purchased an ice cream machine. The Kohr's frozen delicacy had less fat and sugar, which made for a smoother treat. They later improved their machine and refined the recipe. The end result was the original frozen custard. In 1919, the Kohrs opened a small booth on Coney Island and the business took off. There are many tasty flavors to choose from, any two of which can be combined in a twist. Kohr Bros. has five locations on the Ocean City Boardwalk.

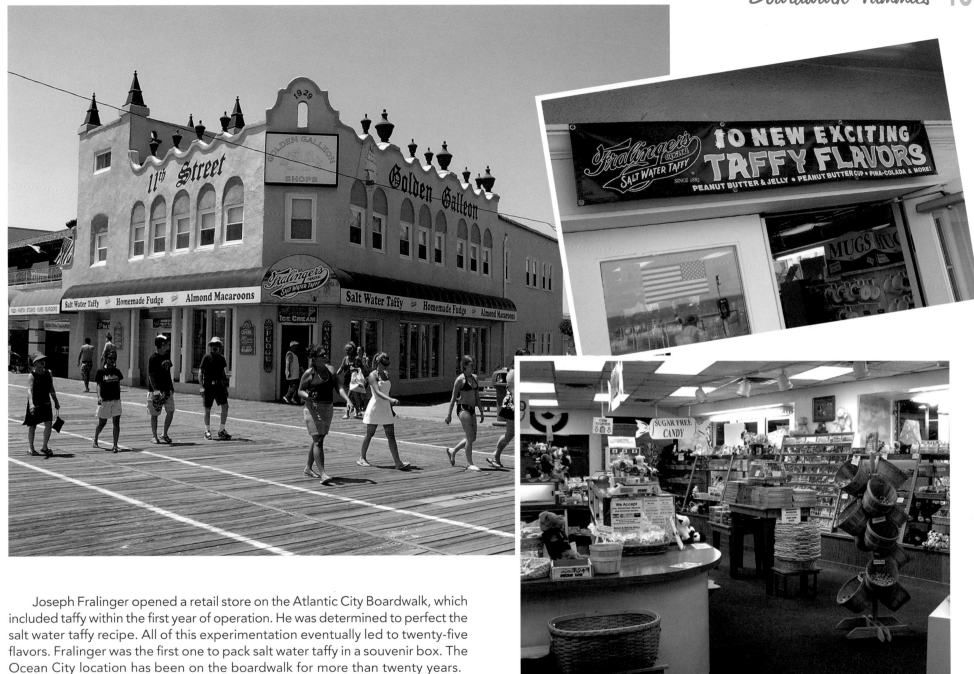

Joseph Fralinger opened a retail store on the Atlantic City Boardwalk, which included taffy within the first year of operation. He was determined to perfect the salt water taffy recipe. All of this experimentation eventually led to twenty-five flavors. Fralinger was the first one to pack salt water taffy in a souvenir box. The Ocean City location has been on the boardwalk for more than twenty years.

Every evening during the beach season a familiar character emerges and greets children of all ages. He's Mr. Peanut and he's a fixture on the boardwalk. Parents stop to take pictures of their children standing next to him to capture that Ocean City moment. The smell of fresh roasted peanuts wafts through the doors of the Boardwalk Peanut Shoppe. Authentic Mr. Peanut collectibles and souvenirs are also available. The Boardwalk Peanut Shoppe Company also handles many of the nut products for the Atlantic City casinos.

Most visitors to Ocean City only encounter the warm and sunny seasons in the town. There's a whole other world of beauty to enjoy if you've never seen the beach and the boardwalk in the winter months.

Photo by Rich Updike

The sea foam freezes along the sand in unique shapes. It may look soft and fluffy, but it is quite the opposite. *Photo by Rich Updike*

The boardwalk during a snowstorm. *Photo by Rich Updike*

The boardwalk after a snowstorm. *Photo by Rich Updike*

Photos by Rich Updike

This photo was actually taken in late December. This guy must really like surfing to brave the icy waters.

Bibliography

Books

Cain, Tim. *Peck's Beach: A Pictorial History of Ocean City, New Jersey*. Harvey Cedars, NJ: Down the Shore Publishing, reprint edition 1993.

Esposito, Frank J. and Robert J. Esposito. *Ocean City, New Jersey*. Charleston, SC: Arcadia Publishing, 1996.

Miller, Fred. *Ocean City: America's Greatest Family Resort*. Charleston, SC: Arcadia Publishing, 2003.

Websites

Boardwalk Peanut Shoppe
www.boardwalkpeanuts.com

The Flanders Hotel
www.theflandershotel.com

Fralinger's Original Salt Water Taffy
www.fralingers.com

Gillian's Wonderland Pier and Waterpark
www.gillians.com

Johnson's Popcorn
www.johnsonspopcorn.com

Kohr Bros. Frozen Custard
www.kohrbros.com

Manco & Manco Pizza
www.mancospizza.com

Ocean City Beach Patrol
www.ocnj.us/ocbp

Ocean City Historical Museum
www.ocnjmuseum.org

Ocean City Music Pier
www.ocnj.us/music-pier

The Ocean City Theaters
www.moorlyn.com

Ocean City Tourism Information
www.ocnj.us

Playland at Castaway Cove
www.boardwalkfun.com

Shriver's Fudge and Salt Water Taffy
www.shrivers.com

Steel's Fudge
www.steelsfudge.com